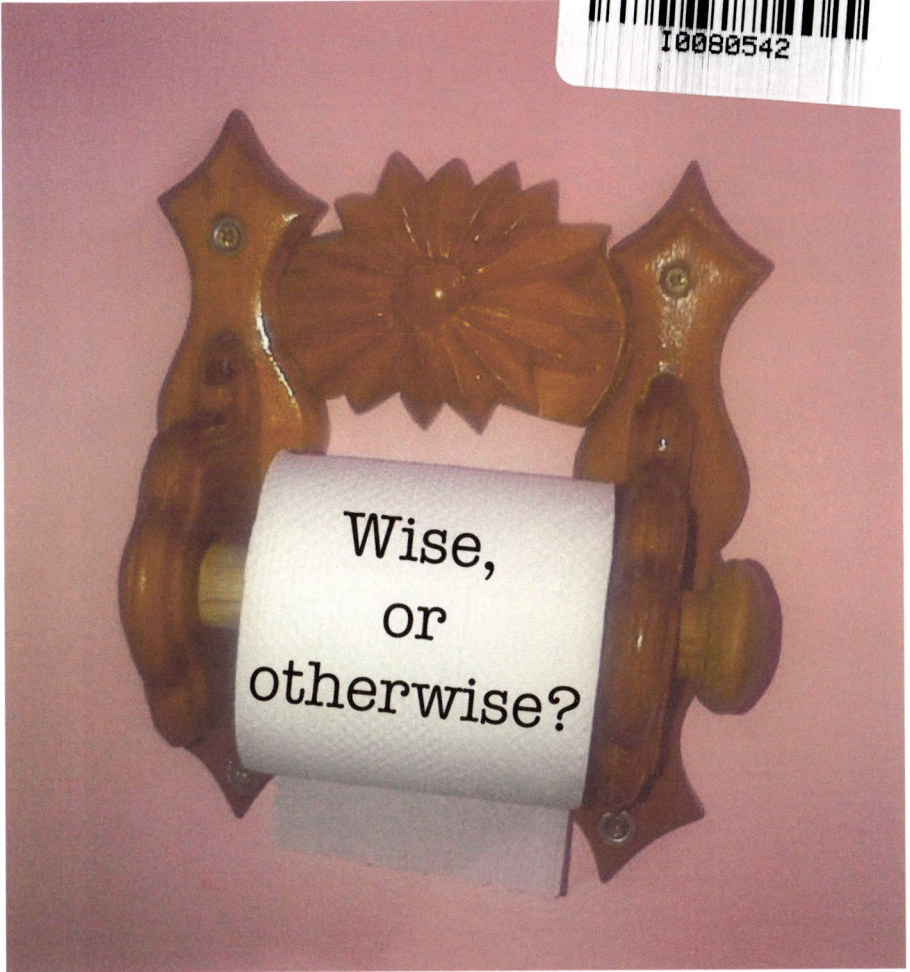

Wise,
or
otherwise?

By Ian Olsen

Wise, or otherwise?

ISBN-13: 978-0-620-76005-8

ISBN-10: 0-620-76005-2

Published by South Africa Writing, Cape Town, Johannesburg

P O Box 717, Rondebosch, 7701, South Africa

info@southafricawriting.com

www.southafricawriting.com

Printed in Cape Town at The Printing Press, Mowbray, South Africa.

Printed worldwide by CreateSpace, Charleston, South Carolina, United States of America.

Two paintings of author, on the front and back cover, painted by Ashley.

Published by:

Corinthia Jordan
380 E. St. Charles #231
Lombard, IL 60148

Text Design by: Djuana Daniel

Illustrations by: Ta'Nia Jordan

ISBN-13: 978-1-949084-01-6

Contents

Part III: Blooming

About the Author

Introduction

Let's just say a planter has a dream of planting a beautiful garden. The planter will first need a space to get things started. It is an important step to determine where exactly should the garden be established. Once the space is secured and the ground deemed fertile, the planter then gets all of the equipment and tools needed to make this dream a reality. The planter then goes to the store to purchase some gardening tools, some seeds (according to the season), a water hose, some gloves, a sun hat, some boots, some pesticide, and some fertilizer. After all the preparation, the planter is ready to begin his garden.

While most see the finished product of the garden as it blossoms in the spring or summer, few recognize the process necessary to produce the results they currently see. The planter will sow seeds coupled with energy and times of observance marking progress. The patience and diligence of the planter usher the manifestation of their dream and a new realm of accomplishment—a new realm of growth.

A flower is beautiful yet delicate. Together, bright petals radiantly bask and reflect the planter's time, hard work and patience. What first begins as a seed, yields a beautiful garden for others to appreciate. Just as each plant goes through a process of implantation, fertilization, germination, and growth, the planter goes through the same process, and they patiently wait to see their expected end.

Flowers are precious because they replicate God's plan for growth in our lives. It all starts with a seed, a passing thought that says, "There has to be more than this," or "I deserve more than this." Growth is not predictable or something to be planned. It is a journey, filled with ups and downs, hills and valleys, happiness and depression, gloomy days and sunny days, days of hope and days of despair. *Life is constant growth*. Through it all, it is our responsibility to balance our need for control with our trust in God's plan for birthing the vision for our lives. It is the difference between self-control and controlling self.

"BLOOM" is a tale of memories dedicated to young women in the process of finding themselves after a time of disappointment or disillusionment. On this path of re-discovery, distractions are inevitable. Blinders meant to save our eyes, compel us to fall prey to deceptions. People we think are for us turn against us; truth hurts but lies somehow heal our insecurities. It is needless to say that life can be a whirlwind. We all have experienced pain at some point in our lives; we all have or will suffer loss. It can be easy to get lost in all of the emotions and powers that come along with those experiences. Nevertheless, it is crucial that we get back to ourselves and never lose sight again. Learning, growing, healing, believing, dreaming, awakening is what this book is all about. This book of poetry is a reminder to all women and young girls that we must go within to find ourselves. We must all stay grounded in this truth, and most of all we must remain true to ourselves.

It is my hope and desire that whether a young girl or a grown woman read these poems, either can learn from my mistakes, heal from my pain and be fearless as they seek the unknown world of "self." As I have borne my soul on these pages, it is a reflection of myself in the hopes that you too will gain the strength and power to *BLOOM* after the rain, and blossom after the storm. The planter has planted the seeds and toiled the ground now he's waiting for us to grow. It's blooming season.

Part I

Seedling

January 22 (Interlude)

Wow, today has been awful. Especially emotionally. I found out the man I love was in love with another and chose her over me. Good for him. Good for them. I was so angry. I didn't know what to do. I called her to let her know what he was doing and when I found out that they were in fact together and that he had been lying to me. I felt like he was using and abusing me. To knowingly withhold information is still lying. I despise liars. I never understood the difficulty with telling the truth. It hurts me that I was delusional, choosing to ignore my gut while dishonoring my heart. I gave. I gave my love too freely. I feel like a raging ocean. I feel unsettled but still safe. I know that to let him go is the best option for me, but I can't help it, it hurts. I could tell he loves her in a way he never loved me. I couldn't understand why. Maybe one day I will.

I also feel like less than the good woman I am for approaching and involving the other woman when she had nothing to do with it. She believed him too. I can't help but feel like this misunderstanding is my fault. I knew he wasn't that into me, but, deep down I thought he'd come around as I fell deeper. I was in too deep. I let my emotions get the best of me. I just want to pass this test. I'm not sure how my actions this time favored me. I just know that I am more than what I'm supposed to be.

I know that I deserve the earth, the moon, the stars and all the starfishes in the sea. I want to be full, so, I can give and give away the best parts of me. I do not even know who I've become. My mother. I don't even know how to tell her. I want to talk to her to let her know about all of the drama I've been causing. Maybe she knows what's best for me. I need her right now. But I'm scared to tell her; I just don't know how. I am writing to feel better, to gain some clarity. My mind needs some rest. I haven't slept in three days, and my back hurts. I need to let go. I need to go home. I need to go home.

What Is It? (Manna)

Why am I here?
What does this all mean?
Everything around me that I can touch
That part of me that I can't seem to take hold of
That ugly part of me that I can't let go of
Take it apart and sew it back up at the seams

If I let you go, promise me you won't go telling the world about me
If I let you go, promise me you won't go telling the world about me

All the secret pain, distant memories, fearless hopes, darkest dreams
Don't let them get to know the best of me
I'd rather live to tell the story for myself
Dressing you up and putting the lies on the shelf
In need of direction, wanting to go right, refusing to go left
Roaming around, seeking freedom, why would I let go of me?

Before the Fall

Wouldn't you love to leave?
I can make you stay
I'd love for you to leave, but
I can make you stay

Bitterness

I saw you on the snap
I saw you were over there
With her and her friends
I saw that you didn't invite me
Clearly didn't make time for me
When it was only time that I needed

I saw the fingers laid across the cards, but
I was the one dealt the bad hand
A queen, no matter how you shuffle the deck
A woman who knows her worth but still settles for less
Growing and learning and loving herself
Keeping, being, seeing, believing that her true love with come

God, I trust you, but if not now, then, when
God, I trust you, but I cannot pretend
That I am okay
Am I okay?
Tired of feeling lonely and afraid
Tired of feeling lost and betrayed

When I'm with the other one
It's a different feel
It's like a cold home that has been abandoned, yet, I still
decided to come in
I still decided to confide
I would rather you be in my life for this moment than to leave
me in this moment, cause
You are real
I know you're afraid of me, but I'm not afraid to let you in
You see right through me even when my eyes conceal
Deep pain that I've only known to feel

I have never felt loved
I have never felt like I belonged anywhere
You welcomed me in and took your time with me

Still holding on even though I can see it's hurting you
I respect that
I know how it feels to love someone who doesn't love you
The cycle repeats itself
We both say I'm not ready yet, but one is always just waiting on
the other
Hoping that one day they will come around to protect and to
honor

Challenges

I don't blame you for changing my name in your phone

I don't blame you for wanting to leave cause the "timing is wrong"

I promise if you stay I won't push you away

I promise if you stay I will make all your fears go away

Bonds

Why do I always believe you?
It's like your word is my truth
And to deny you of your power would feel ungodly and unruly

Why can't I let go of you?
Your presence makes me feel assured
I'm all you need but when you're gone the loss doesn't
complete me

Why can't I leave you?
Trapped in a blissful daze, sitting here lost in this maze
Confused at the way you looked when you said I felt like home

Isn't that what we're all searching for?
That other human being who makes us feel at home

Why then are you traveling?
When you're away, I can still feel you
As you break our pact and break our bond

Why haven't I left you too?
And it would feel good to do to you what you've done to me
I deserve the world at large, but I accepted your, "I am not
ready yet" to ease my anxieties

Why won't you make my dreams come true?

As I reflect on this mess that I've allowed myself to be in
It's sad to say that I still choose you.

Solstice

I want to tell you all the crazy things that go on in my mind
The things that stay in my mind until you're here
Your presence is my peace that's why I'm afraid when you're not near

All power. I don't think you know your power

I don't think you know the way you ease my mind
When you are lifting me up, and we are taking it slow
On this long road, and this turn has been slow

In circles. We have been going in circles

You're afraid that I might actually want to stay
I'm afraid that in my mind is where you lay all day
You're afraid that I won't let you walk away

Teach me. How to not be afraid

But you like it this way
So, I choose to stay quiet
Letting you run my mind while your heart is on silent

Selfish

Honestly,
I just want love. Real, Unconditional, God-like Love.

Wonderlust

I wonder how wide she ripped your heart open
I wonder if you have the strength to love again
I wonder if you are still in love with her
I wonder if you've forgiven yourself
I wonder how it feels to be loved by me
I wonder if you'll ever get over what happened to you
I wonder if I'll ever get over what happened to me
I wonder if you know that I'll wait for you to heal as I am healing too
I wonder how long?
I wonder if you will love me hard
I wonder if she plumaged your rib when she took your heart
I wonder if you've seen God
I wonder how long we will last before you start to trust me
I wonder why you still like me
I wonder how long?
I wonder if you're selling me dreams long enough to make me stay
I wonder if our children will have your face
I wonder where I fit in your vision
I wonder if you really love me
I wonder if I can make you better
I wonder if you're really into me
I wonder how much you pray about me
I wonder if your friends know you love me
I wonder if you really love me
I wonder how long?
I wonder what our song will be
I wonder if we could build a house and turn it into a home
I wonder if you see your future with me
I wonder if the high will burn out and you'll burn the ashes too
I wonder if you know your strengths and weaknesses

I wonder if you're ready yet
I wonder if I can give you what you need
I wonder if you're mine
I wonder how long?

Messages

I dreamt of a snail crawling up my leg
Begging me to pick him up
I saw his reflection in the mirror as I looked up above my bed

I wish I could have let you all the way in
I wish my thoughts wouldn't lead me to sin
I wish this dungeon weren't so comfortable or I might let you in

Darkness is only evaded by the light
Tongue wrestling and we're in between
Loves high, come on in I'll love to fight

Influenced by a mediocre peasant, misusing my muse
Afraid to shine, so I'm abusing my palette
Secrets so true that God bless the only few that knew

Messages from a broken man, telling me he wants me to be his queen
Boy, don't you know I'm not used to that!
I'm used to being a hit it and quit it take you home to mama
Make you feel like I feel it

Messages to my broken friends, don't love that man

Meaningless

Broken, bruised, heartless, molded
Unbreakable, misguided, mended, soulful
Redeemed, healed, tested, chosen.

Thieves

The thief comes not but to destroy, steal, and kill
Some crushed, some separated, others plow
Undisputed territory, my mind's the mill

You came in the form of a man
The man of my dreams
Seemed like it was destined to be

When I woke up
The wet pillow let me know that enough was enough
I was never enough

Family, hopes, dreams, memories
I let it all go in hopes of what we could be
In hopes of finding parts of me

Parts of me were left scattered, beyond my mental unrest
To the north, to the east, to the south, and to the west
I was the only one to blame for this timely mess

So, little by little, brick by brick,
I build this wall of defense, where my treasures will not rot or
rust
And no thief will ever get in

Cycles

I know when you're lying
I know when you're tired of trying
We made a promise to lift each other up
Front to front back to back
Alone in a wolf pack
I'm afraid to need you
Scared broken
Two individuals who are broken
Can you love me in my brokenness?
Or will you run from my disgusting mess
I allowed you to come into
My temple
Ladies love you, but I see straight through you
Maybe you want me too
Maybe you're alone like me but just like my mental
What is going on up there?
You ask me even though you are fully aware
Just read me
Look at the blank expression in my eyes
The fake curl of my lips when I smile
The slight tilt of my head to show I'm listening
When I'm not
I'm thinking about where you're going and with who
And why wasn't I invited

And when will you ask me to marry you

Is marriage even on your mind

Do you even like me

Do you want a house or a condo, six rooms or three

Were you really at home last night or were you laid up with the woman who is less than me?

But I nod my head and say, "Okay baby, I understand"

We are going in circles, I tell you

And you laugh. You never listened to

Anything I said

Sounds familiar

Words of a legend

If that man don't do you right

Then baby don't let him; don't sweat him

Just forget him and tell him

This young queen is gonna be alright

This young queen is gonna be just fine

This young queen will be alright

Joules

Let's keep this just between you and me
We exchange a sacred energy
We intersect more than just physically
Cell memory
Divine chemistry

Desire

More than seeing your face every morning

More than holding you after you have a bad dream

More than kissing you with my morning breath

More than calling you in the middle of the day to see how you're doing

More than falling asleep on the phone with you—scared that I'll miss your breath

More than holding hands starring deeply into your brown eyes

More than caressing the lines of your smile

More than listening when you talk about your dreams, your hopes, your passions

More than missing you when I am away

More than leaving you, wishing you'd stay

More than your skin

More than your scent

More than hugging you goodbye

More than your lies

More than the truth that lies behind your eyes

More than wanting what's best for you, even if it's not me

More than knowing that it is me

More than believing everything you told me

More than just you and I you see

More than our selfish ways and animosity

More than killing myself and losing the old me

More than life

More than death

More than heaven and hell

More than time

More than spells

Seasons

My favorite sweater from last fall doesn't fit me anymore. My shoes don't fit either. Wonder if my crown still fits the same too. I trusted you. With all my lies, my mess. The same empty thoughts that depleted my success. We were both messes. Stuck in the mud. No sticks. No water. No wicks. Just wax. Just bliss.

Capsules

From my well, you came and drank. Lowered your barrel to constantly relieve your heartache. My mistake.

This time around things will be different. The well is deeper. The uphill battle is steeper; the wounds heal deeper.

Fresh springs, poplar trees, wind breeze, mind's at ease. Sin is just a tease.

So, I'll strip for you; we both know where that line is. We never crossed it, not now, nor then.

We're older now; times are changing. Rules are breaking. Seasons have been changing. Intentions rearranging.

Our time and our space are near the end. Time up. The clock is still on the wall, but your time is up.

Beautiful and Broken

The most beautiful part of you is the part you haven't let go of. It is the image that you are afraid of. The reflection in the mirror reveals what you are truly made of.

Reflections don't lie, mirrors do. Some seek the lie but end up in truth. So, fly high and do you. Be good and good will come to you. Be light and let it shine through. Head up high; a king is watching you. Smile wide; God is in you.

Scattered

If I am you and you are me, then we are in deep trouble. Mad, sick, gone. When I look into your eyes, I see palm trees. Life's good and such a breeze. When I look into your heart I see hopes and dreams, fears and admirations, look what you did to me. When I look into your soul, I see titanium hiding pure gold. I see darkness dispersed by light. I feel love, being held in the night. I hear lies in the face of truth. I hear you loudly knocking when you want some attention. I smell you loud, baby, what else are we missing.

Closure

I am seeking closure because I'm tired of choosing between what feels right and what feels true

I am seeking closure because I know you're here for this moment and you don't plan to stay

I am seeking closure because I deserve the love that I've been dying to give you

I am seeking closure because I want real love to come and the pain to fade away

I am seeking closure because you only needed me when she didn't need you

Leaving

I don't know which I like better—
The sound of the wind that slammed the door behind me
Or the taste of salt on your lips after you kissed me goodbye

Part II

_____

Budding

Psycho

Last night was a liberating experience

I came home after a night of homework and free breakfast

Quality time spent with a friend

I lit a candle to get a dose of the islands

I undressed, freeing myself from that heavy mess

I didn't shower because I was exhausted

I laid alone in my bed restless because no one was next to me

I texted my number two now number one because my main has been ignoring me for his number two

How rude

He couldn't make it either

I was cool it that

I laid topless almost bottomless

Fighting thoughts of depression and anxiety telling me I'm no good

Then I remembered what the preacher said in service that morning

I said a simple prayer thanking God for His peace

His perfect peace

I immediately felt His presence surround me and protect me

In that moment I knew not to be afraid

I knew not to feel betrayed by anyone or anything

I took what was given to me and decided to create and live the life He had for me

I realized I was not in control of things

As I let go
Liberty came
I let go of fear
I let go of past mistakes
I let go of heartbreak and heartache
I decided to love and to be me
I decided that from this day forward I would be me.

Flesh and Blood

My mind has been spinning, barely winning
Fulfilling sins I would never reveal to my mother
Skillfully betraying my lover. Selfishly giving
Leaving out the best parts of me. Afraid
To show you the real me.

Battling in the realm of the heavenlies
Almost lost myself. Each lesson brings
Strength. An enemy who doesn't truly know
Any better. Should I feel that I am
Better. Best yet. The worst is yet
To come.

Pleasures

I self-medicate to alleviate everything that suffocates me
I meditate to reflect on the dreadful dreams I hope to reach

Floating

Learning that it's the strong ties rather than your long strides
that has kept me on this ride

Learning that it's my high hopes rather than your deep strokes
that has kept me afloat

Learning that it's you that has held me down and turned my life
upside and inside out

Exceptions

I thought love meant acceptance
So, I gladly made the exception for you
I thought love meant forgiveness
So, I reluctantly prayed to release me from you
I thought love meant freedom
So, I willingly allowed myself to let go of you

Patience

Some things just take time
No one wakes up and suddenly has it all together
So, go back to sleep and wait for better.

Time

Constantly Changing

Rapidly Rearranging

Steadily Swaying

Effortlessly Evolving

Eternity's Engaging

Abundantly Abiding

Fiercely Flowing

Secretly Succeeding

Willingly Waiting

Tactfully Treasuring

Patiently Painting

Hastily Healing

Beautifully Bathing

Courageously Craving

Dangerously Dating

Carefully Creating

Peacefully Pacing

Skillfully Separating

Generously Gravitating

Initially Innovating

Tastefully Tasting

Lost

If we could live in this moment, it would show us that time doesn't exist.

Instead, we would find ourselves wrapped up in the abyss.

We would be falling deep.

We would have the world at our feet.

Envious of our love.

All to learn that it was fake.

You and I are not real.

We do not exist, and this was all a lie that we made up in our heads.

A mental pixel that became reality.

Someone get me out of here.

She wishes she could tell her daddy.

But he's not here.

Unlike you, he left because he knew he was no good.

He didn't want to nurture a seed and lose his head when he realized it was perfect.

A reflection of the night that she was made.

He didn't know that she would need him when life was weird.

Now she's falling into the deep throat of sin.

Lonely

In those uncomfortable times, you are the one I call
When I am too afraid to face myself, I used you to fill the space

It was in those weary times when I felt like I needed you the most
You were never there

In those blissful times, I was stripped down and broken bare to my core
When I needed to be revealed, you allowed me to heal

It was in those disgusting times when I felt I needed you the most
You were always there

Blessings

Little girl, why do you continue to make these same old mistakes

You will learn, and you will see that time is not your only enemy

You will learn, and you will lead

Those who don't know the blessing it is to feel so deep

Depths (Feelings)

We are all here on this huge rock filled with water

We are all made up of the same water, the same dirt, but we throw rocks at each other

We are all here

We are on this ride together

We are building something greater

We are all alone together

We are gone and going to be gone for a very long time

We are going in circles and circles you see under my eyes after you return from your trip days Upon weeks you left me, and now I see your face again

We are together

We are here

We are lying in my sheets that my other lover has lain in while you were gone

We are faithful to each other and loyal to our commitment issues

We are gone

We are rising

We are in the maze together, but we will make it out

We are in love

We are alive

We are reaching for new heights and new discoveries of each other

We are together

We are here

We are in the midst of something new that feels old

We are gathering the pieces of the puzzle that we set out to solve a while ago when I was sick

We are sore

We are one

We are two

We are alike but different the parts of you i love are the parts of myself i hate

We are young

We were free

We are found

We are going

We are together

We are here

We are in tune

We are consumed by what they think

We are immune to kindness

We are immune to the looks

We are just because we don't need to ask permission

We are in love

We are in love

We are together and in love

Rare

I cut off the one I love the most after two years because I wasn't ready to deal when shit got too real.

Petty

I wonder how you Feel
Now knowing you were all I ever wanted.

I've got someone better
Now and he's not afraid to own it.

Resentment

I was going to send you a message saying how much I hated you. Then I realized that it would only be a waste of time, a waste of energy. No more would I give you all that I had to offer because it would never be good enough. No more would I consider myself not good enough. I am more than enough. So, while you're out with your friends who I have never met, I wish you happiness and joy and peace. It seems like you need them more than me.

Being

You are allowed to exist in this time and in this space.

You are allowed to be present and use this gift to connect with others.

You are allowed to be happy, to be sad, to feel joy, to be glad.

You are allowed to be the best or be the worse.

You are allowed to know yourself before discovering someone else.

You are allowed to play by your own rules.

You are allowed to be fearless.

You are allowed to say no.

You are allowed to press pause.

You are allowed to have late starts.

You are allowed to be imperfect.

You are allowed to see.

You are allowed to touch.

You are allowed to hear.

You are allowed to smell.

You are allowed to taste.

You are allowed to be.

Freedom

Ready to settle, ready to relate
Tired of going down this same long road
With this longing in my soul
Wondering if you're the reason why I left him in the first place
Deep feelings and longings of you, my muse
Only you can unhook and untie these screws
Just come in
Work with your hands take all the time you need
Give me the chance to heal I'm in need
Give me the chance to dry eyes and bleed
Sacrifice, love is here no need to roll the dice
I'd bet it all, give it all for you just to hold you
Put your mind to rest
Can't you see, baby, it was all just a test
I wasn't afraid to lose you
That's why you're here because I choose you

After all, we revealed our deepest Enemies
Our soul's regrets
Thankful that you're here
I'm yours but let's take it easy
Let's make it easy
Just give me all of you
Let my love protect you
Let our love correct them
Let the lies be overcome with fear
Let's take this spliff
Hope you can see what I see
Don't close your eyes
Listen and read

Quick Trip

I put aside my mental temperament
Used my mind to circumvent my world
What I see is only a quick dream
It's like I'm tied in the in-between
It's like this ride you're on with me
It's like I want to move forward and see where this could go
It's like I want you
Don't know what else to say but I want you
Here with me right now, whenever you're free
That's when you're with me
That's what I like to see
That's what I love in me
You're still here
Not close but here
Not down but here
Lifted but here

Venus

My balance, my peace

Space and time fill my distant memories

The days we'd run and escape this myth

This myth of love

Growth

I was there when it mattered most
I gave you my love, and still, you would boast
That you did it on your own
I was the one that crowned you when you came to the throne
Left you sheltered, clothed you, spoke life to your dry bones

I gave you life
With every bit of me, I chose to fulfill all the qualities of a wife
Despite you being none of that for me
Now I'm left feeling broken and empty
I'm glad it wasn't meant to be

Part III

_____

Blooming

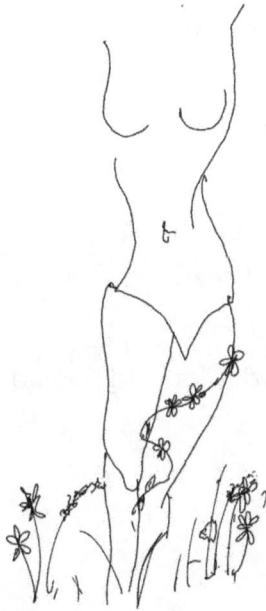

Creation

In the beginning, there you were
With me in all of my mess
You created the heavens and the earth in seven days,
Yet, I am still incomplete
You watch, and you show me
How simple it all could be
If I just let go and trust
Forsaking all the pleasures that filled my eyes with lust
Disgust, you must feel for your daughter
But your love reminds me that I am stronger
No longer
Will I believe the lies, the perceptions that cloud my mind
Instead, I'll take what you have given me,
Stroke the ego and destroy the lesser me
Nurture and fulfill destiny
Create legacy
I let go of past mistakes
I let go of heartbreak and heartache
I decided to love and to be me
I decided that from this day forward I would be me.

Sole

Hidden behind all of these layers
Took a while for me to see what I was truly made of

More than just skin, organs, tissues, and cells
More than just hopes, fears, dreams, and nightmares

Time separated me from the bounds that held my soul
confined
What lied inside was too deep to be found

Renaming

You are not defined by what you feel
You are not defined by what you desire to be
You are defined by what you choose to see.

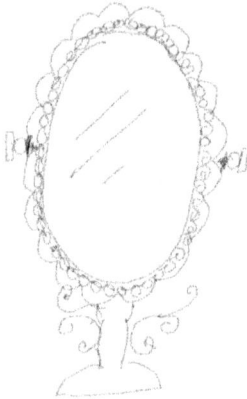

Enough

For years I've battled with feelings of despair
The voice inside my head warned me to always be prepared
To always be first, but it was no surprise that I didn't listen

Until I found that everything I needed was already inside of me
I realized I had the power to mold and co-create my reality
It was then that I began to see the God in me

My old reflections began to crumble
Broken glass cut my inner wounds deeper
The pain was felt deeper, but still

I climbed that mountain of self-love even when it got steeper
In the end, the salt from my tears cleansed me
I was found. I knew that I was the keeper

Being (Part II)

As
This
Beautiful
Being
That
You
Have
Created
To
Live
In
This
Deep
Brown
Skin,
Help
Me
To
Keep
My
Peace
And
Not
Be
Controlled
By
Men.

Timeless

If the present is a gift
Then unwrap me with delight

Don't take off my covering swiftly
Take your time and do it slowly

Grow to nourish me
Speak to replenish me

If the present is a gift
Then I am forever timeless

Don't eat until your stomach is glad
Take your time and eat with your soul instead

Learn to appreciate me
Love to cultivate me

Beauty

I've always felt like I wasn't good enough to be held for a
lifetime
But lifetimes have passed, and I'm still here holding
All the treasures that have been planted inside of me

I've been hidden out of the light so that I couldn't see
The passing dangers and distractions that come from men
I didn't realize that you were protecting me

Thank you for guiding me.

Peace

When you can turn your frustration into fixtures of appreciation.
When you can reason with your demons out of demonstrations.

Well Wishes

I have waited for this sensation to pass
They told me to feel it, embrace it, accept it, learn from it

I've let you go because you didn't belong
I realized that I wasn't your home
I contain a sacred space that doesn't belong to you

You will never understand me
I create chemistry, a master of alchemy
I turned this lead that was meant to poison me into gold

You, baby, even still are solid gold.

Raw

I have learned that everything is not always about me.
The pain that I feel is for a greater purpose.
To heal me, my family. For future generations to come
They are all I need.
I've been scared straight onto the path to my destiny.
I no longer search for home in other bodies.
I am home. I have God inside of me.
She is all I need.

Finding God

It was in the crippling silence

The chirps of birds I had no knowledge of

The gushes of winds I knew not from where they came or where they were going

It was the alone time I spent counting the days before I would enter my paradise

It was the hopes and dreams that you placed inside of me

It was the sacrifices my forefathers and present guides made

It was life's simplicities and death's complexities

It was the moments I sat in confusion wondering why you created me this way

It was me cherishing the very moments that took my breath away

It was the smile on that motherless child's face that pushed me to keep going when I didn't have a clear destination in mind

It was the hope that I could be someone; it was the fact that I am someone

Someone beautiful and unique and irreplaceable and weirdly distinct

It was the idea that you, the Almighty thought of me

(Un)forgiveness

I have within me
The grace to be
Delicate and raunchy

I have within me
The strength to be
Comfortable in my solidarity

I have within me
The power to be
Brave in times in uncertainty

I have within me
The power to be
Set free

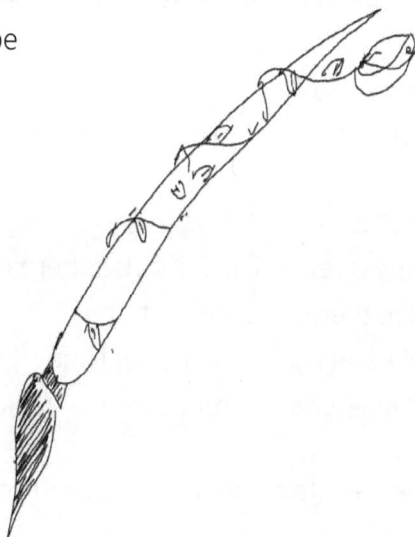

Bonds (Part II)

And I would choose you again and again
Even when the ties are loose
Even when the time is good
Why am I here again
Same cycles, same seasons, same indecisive reasons of why I
let you back in
Isn't that what love is all about
Accepting, forgiving, sacrificing, and bending over backwards
for unreciprocated efforts
Just slaps on the ass when you've given and given all of your
sacred energy for a man that is still half empty
But I like it
Cause I feel like you need me
And apparently, I need you to make me feel needed
Hoping for better days when you'll appreciate me
I love even the worse of you
Hoping for our time to be uninterrupted by distractions that are
no good for me
Or too good for you
Dreams reveal my insecurities or maybe alternate realities
Either way, you're there, and I'm hurting
In pain because I don't feel worthy, but I know I am
My mother raised a queen so how dare you make me feel less
than
How dare you come into my world and assert yourself, king
Without recognizing your queen
I can see clearly now my eyes have been opened

Lies

Reflections don't lie, mirrors do
So, when you look at me, all you see is the truth

Mirrors

You are my light as I travel through space
I get lost, but you always make a way
You are my tool as I navigate through Hades

You hold the keys that I need
I fight the powers, so they can't hold me
You are that fire that purifies me

You show me where I need to go next
I scream and yell for Poseidon, but he doesn't hear me
You help me find God when I am lost at sea

BeLoved

I am loved

I am valued

I am more than what you see

I am the essence of time and space built upon one body

I am true to my being

I am divine

I am more than what you see

I am different from last year

I am seen as a force to be reckoned with

I am the truth in the presence of power

I am more than what you see

I am grateful to be here

I am grateful for this life I have been given

I am me

I am more than what you see

I am the vision you dreamed in times past

I am your greatest fears

I am your most pleasant memories

I am more than what you see

Wild Flower

We choose our comfortable "un-comfortability"

Even when we didn't have a clue
Even when our hearts and our actions leave you

Wanting more of you, giving less of me
Wandering, stuck in the in-between

Wondering will you love me in my mess?
Why, oh God, did you choose to give me the burden of unrest?

Feet planted, eyes forward, heart, broken
Forced to believe that I am still the chosen

I am your child, planted in the wild
Blossoming beautifully under the tall oak tree

Planted by the waters,
Still, deep clean waters

Graciously feeding me

Muse

Creation has an order
You're trapped in this chaos
And he's amused by your irresponsibility to apply the principle
of reciprocity

What goes up must come down
Except you as you're running downtown
Relieving the pain, scattered away, afraid of what traps you in
the escape

You were created in His image and after His likeness,
How dare you ever misuse your power
Letting him have your power

You wanted a prince to tell you to let down your hair
As he used your crown as an entryway to what laid ahead
Only to realize you wouldn't go far beyond what laid ahead

Looking for the player's token before he enters your realm
Saving you from that evil joker
That man didn't turn out to be Batman; I guess you had to
learn instead

Your hair would never be long enough
Your skin would never be fair enough
Your hips would never be wide enough

Creation has an order
He wasn't part of the plan
You're older and wiser now, with a rock on both hands

Time (Part II)

We have access to your hands but
We do not control
The true power
That comes from within

Selene

Not to be mistaken with Venus, the goddess of love
You, my love, are the ruler of the moon

With strong tides, you sway the emotions of your child
You quickly remind all who wander, of the pain and sorrows of their sins

Every morning and every night you show us the meaning of rebirth
You keep us sane, staying afloat in the oceans of this earth

MVP

It was in the night that I found the light I needed
It was in my pain that I found the prince of peace

It was in the valley that I found the strength to proceed
It was in my brokenness that I found my most valuable piece

Practices

Sometimes, it is not what you do,

But it is always what you say

Over and over

In your mind

To yourself

That makes the difference.

Practice over time makes you different

Treasures

Sometimes, it's the smile in your eyes that makes me come alive and the peace I've found cannot be denied.

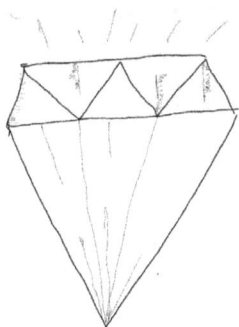

Eight Ten Eleven (Ships)

While I was wandering, you kept me anchored
You reminded me that I was settling
When I was low, you helped me raise my standard

Without you, I am lost at sea,
Drowning in my fears and my doubts
In the storm, you remained my peace

My home, my refuge, I know that I am safe
When I couldn't see, you wiped my eyes clean
No judgment, just a vagabond, a proud waif

You showed me the path that leads home
Guided me by the still waters
My God, Jehovah Shalom

Baby Girl,

He could never love you with an empty heart and broken trust.

Agreement

Give me your loyalty, and I'll give you my love

Give me your dream, and I'll help build it up

Give me your seed, and I'll supply the soil

Give me your sign, and I'll hold the pole

Give me your mission, and I'll complete it

Give me your time, and I'll give you a treasure

Give me your mind, and I'll do you one better

My Love

You are never alone dear
For I am forever here

Peace (Part II)

It is better to wait and watch the ship as it sets sails than to
walk away then turn back when it's too late

Good Riddance

I am sorry that I wasn't patient enough with you
Didn't want to wait on you
Time was getting the best of me and you
I gave my very best to you

Still Learning

Now that we're friends
I see you differently

I see that you are not like me
You are your own

You are coming into your own
Still learning

Forgive me for not understanding,
For trying too hard to control

What was not meant to be
I am still learning

Deadlines

What happens if the highs never balance out the lows?

GOD

Complicated. Our feelings. Sweet
Dealings
I was dealt the right hand at the wrong time

Emasculated. The feminine. Timely
Balance
It is our savior that keeps us alive

Alignment

Time does not exist in the ancient realms
Where monkeys, lions and bears are equal
When the mind was spirit and used to redeem simple people
Who cast those spells, who told you that you were unequal?

Too Good

What is not meant to be will always feel good to the flesh

This flesh and this blood is the only thing that separates us

Don't be afraid to dive deeply; the ocean belongs to you

heARTwork

Do your job and release them
Let them be happy as you desire to be
We all deserve that luxury, right?
Maybe they needed it more than me

Sincerity

Sweet peace,

Thank you for keeping me

Reminding me to see

The chaos and the fall

The rise and the call

The beauty of it all

Rules of Engagement

I am more than what you see
The essence of my being is what drives me
Zoe is the force that guides me

I am present
I am still
I am strong

The fine lines that eliminate the beauty of my smile
Hold me back
It lifts and carries me beyond what I can even imagine or see

I am beautiful
I am aware
I am gentle

Beautifully designed, uncontrollably confined to the Divine
Smitten, released, cruise control on repeat
Afraid to press repeat, it no longer serves me

I am hopeful
I am sound
I am open

LOVE

Pieces of me
I give
All I have
My very best

The time we spent
Painful
Never forget
Timeless

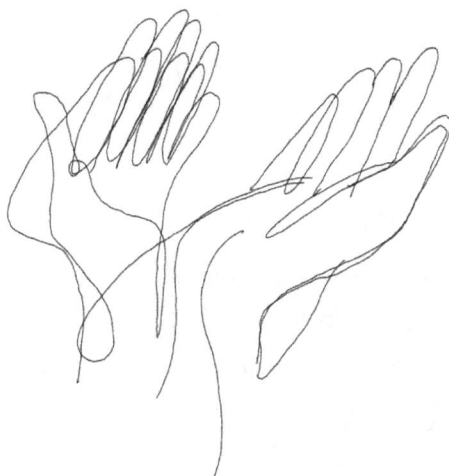

Take my last
I give
You my first,
My very last

New Beginnings

Planted being watered
Growing from the roots being
Watered budding being
Watered grow leaves being
Watered bloom in season
Being watered die
Remains come together
To decompose and be
Born again into
Something new and ever
More beautiful

With Love,

Corinthia

About the Author

Corinthia Jordan is a journalist studying Mass Communications at Southern Illinois University Edwardsville. She started writing poetry as a means of self-reflection and healing and later with the hope that it would be a vehicle to help others. Her poetry debut, titled "Mas'r Peace," was published in the 2017 edition of the *River Bluff Review*, an annual literary magazine hosted by Southern Illinois University Edwardsville. Her blog, *Corinthia Jordan*, is an outlet where she expresses her thoughts on promoting education, self-love, self-awareness, and spirituality. It is her mission to serve others by using her words to uplift, heal, and inspire.

www.ingramcontent.com/pod-product-compliance
Lightning Source LLC
LaVergne TN
LVHW051809080426
835513LV00017B/1873